I Know I Can!
Omelette On Toast

ANTHEA DAVIDSON-JARRETT

Illustrated by

Aldana Penayo

Published by EDUCATE THE GLOBE,
London, UK, 2020.

ISBN: 978-1-913804-04-6

Copyright © 2020 Educate The Globe Limited. All rights reserved. No part of this book is to be reprinted, copied or stored in retrieval systems of any type, except by written permission from the author. Part of this book may, however, be used only in reference to support related documents or subjects.

I know I can do it!

Please can I help?

I want to do it all by myself!

Please can I try?

Can you show me how?

I'm not too small;

I am ready right now!

I've just come home from school

and I am feeling hungry.

What can I eat?

Something big and chunky!

My brother says he will

help me cook a meal.

I think that I can do it;

bring it on! What's the deal?

Omelette on toast

will do just fine.

Grab some eggs; let's have

a tasty teatime!

We need mushrooms and salt;

red onions and black pepper.

Ooh! Omelettes are great

with a little shredded cheddar!

Chop! Chop! Chop!

Slice! Slice! Slice!

This is what mummy does

when she makes fried rice!

I have to be careful

when I crack the eggs.

Take out the shells;

try not to make a mess!

Whisk! Whisk! Whisk!

Everything together.

Add some mixed herbs

so that it tastes better.

Pour a drop of milk

into the mix.

Whisk! Whisk! Whisk!

I'm really good at this!

Get the frying pan;

melt butter in it.

Pour the mixture in...

it will be ready in a minute!

Now for the bread!

It needs toasting.

Make sure you keep checking

so it doesn't start burning!

If you use an oven

make sure to turn it over

so both sides can be

crispy and golden!

Now the toast is ready; time to spread the butter.

Ask mummy if she wants her food with a hot cuppa.

Now lay the omelette

over the toast then

do the washing-up so

mum can make pot roast.

It's teatime

and it tastes so good!

I would definitely eat this

everyday if I could!

Making omelettes is easy

now I know how.

Thanks big bro!

Let's finish these plates now!

www.ingramcontent.com/pod-product-compliance
Lightning Source LLC
Chambersburg PA
CBHW041245240426
43670CB00027B/2992